Purrfect
English

Paw-ket Dictionary
Cat to Human

JILLIAN BLUME

CENTENNIAL BOOKS

Purrfect English

Paw-ket Dictionary
Cat to Human

Contents

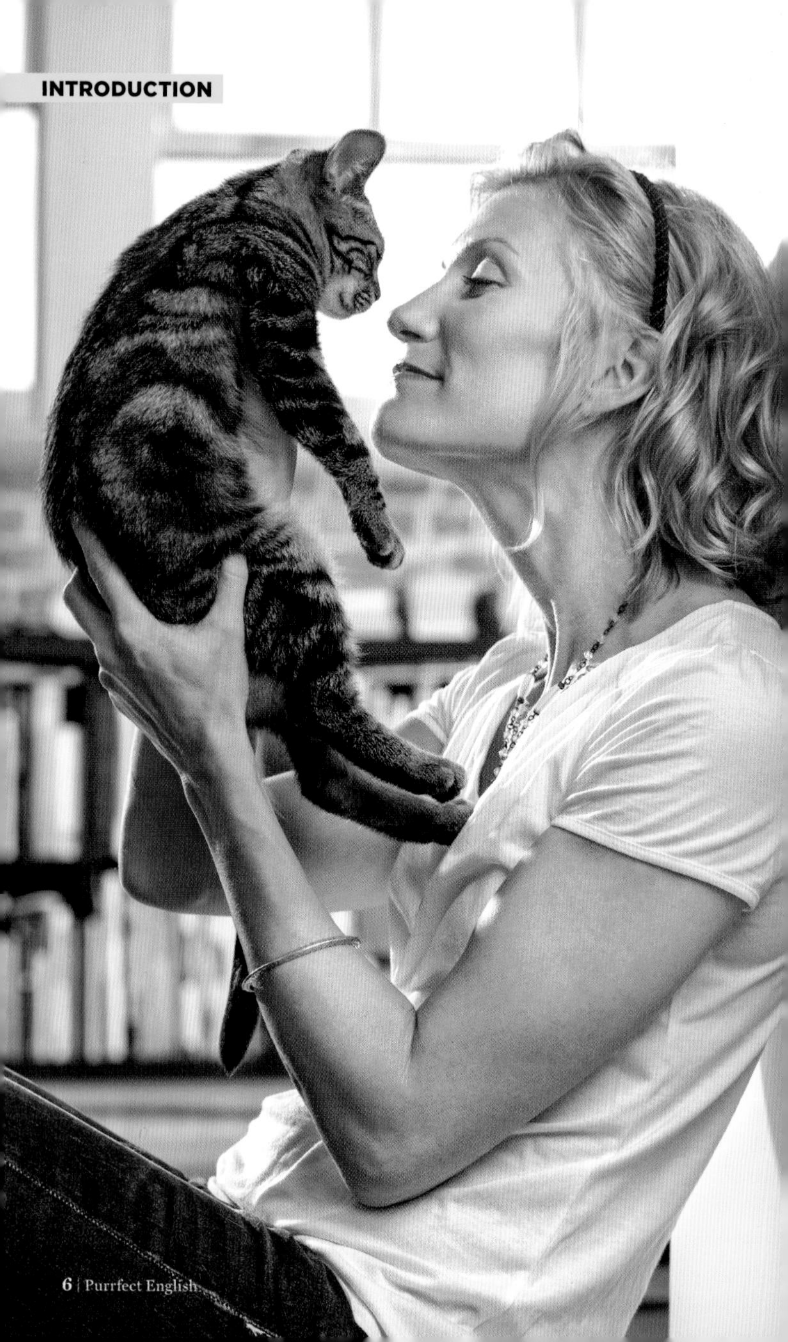

Can You Speak Cat?

Scientists, veterinarians and animal behaviorists focusing on the mysterious world of cats are providing some insight into the minds of our feline companions.

We are a nation of ailurophiles, aka cat lovers: Over 58 million felines live as family members in our homes; another 30 million to 40 million cats serve as neighborhood ambassadors or pest-control workers in warehouses, breweries and bars, and are cared for by legions of kitty admirers. Yet in spite of these numbers, cats are still seen as aloof, wild and enigmatic creatures.

The fact is that cats—while highly independent—have the capacity to love their human families. Research has shown that not only are they capable of forming deep bonds with bipeds, they have their own intricate methods of communication using vocalizations, body language and specific actions. Cats have even developed a vocabulary of meows to communicate primarily with humans—but there's a lot more to learning to "speak cat" than mere meowing.

While we love our animals and shower them with affection (and treats), the most meaningful gift we can give our felines is to understand what they are trying to tell us. This book aims to familiarize cat owners with the basic definitions of their pets' multifaceted communication and behavior, and provide essential tips to help keep our furry friends healthy and happy from kittenhood to their golden years.

There's a lot to discover. You'll find out about how cats communicate with their eyes; the meaning of their squeaks, hisses, yowls, trills and other vocalizations; their many stages of development; what makes a cat "feral"; felines' superpower senses of hearing and smell; why and how cats mark; and even how to train your pet to give you a high five.

Whether your cats are zooming around the house in the dark, rubbing up against your leg or chatting at the bird just outside the window, there's a lot going on that they want you to know about. Flip through this A–Z guide to learn their language (it's easier than you may think!) and provide your furry friend with a life full of love and enrichment.

—Jillian Blume

Acrobatic
(a-krə-ˈba-tik)

As descendants of hunters that must seek out their prey, cats are quick, powerful, flexible and agile. Their supple spines are composed of flexibly connected vertebrae with highly elastic cushioned disks between them, which allows them to perform their acrobatic feats. They can right themselves in midair and land on their feet—thus the saying "Cats have nine lives"—but if they fall from great heights, they're just as likely to suffer injuries, so windows should always be fitted with secure screens.

Who Knew?

A cat's shoulder blades attach to muscles, not bones, which makes their front halves highly flexible.

A

Adoption
(ə-ˈdäp-shən)

To take a cat by choice into a relationship—and the generally preferred method of finding a new kitten or adult cat for your family. The best shelters have guidelines for weaning, vaccinating and spaying or neutering cats before adoption (or perform those services), and their fees are much less than the cost of buying a cat from a breeder. While you're there, consider getting a pair of feline friends: Bonded pairs can keep each other company and are less likely to exhibit signs of boredom or anxiety.

Who Knew?

Approximately 3.2 million shelter animals are adopted each year (1.6 million dogs and 1.6 million cats), according to the American Society for the Prevention of Cruelty to Animals (ASPCA).

B

Black Cats

('blak 'kats)

The myth that black cats are unlucky may have started because people used to trip over them in the dark! The Japanese, on the other hand, believe it's a good omen if one crosses your path. A black cat on your doorstep in Scotland means money is coming your way. In Celtic folklore, the black cat Sith is a witch who transforms into a cat nine times (hence the "nine lives" idea). Popular breeds of black cats include the Bombay, a favorite in India, which looks like a jungle cat but is actually a loving lap cat.

Who Knew?

The image of a witch with a black cat took hold in the Middle Ages when Pope Gregory IX denounced cats as evil and in league with Satan.

Blind

('blīnd)

Sightless. All kittens are born blind (and deaf), so they rely on their mother's warmth and vocalization to nurse. During the first two weeks after birth, the mother will tend to her kittens, which will double in size and their eyes will finally open so they can look around. But adult cats' eyes are also vulnerable to injury and diseases that can impair their eyesight or even create partial or total blindness, so watch for potential vision problems (especially in middle-aged or senior cats), as early intervention can help prevent vision loss.

Who Knew?

Kittens' eyes are part of the nervous system, which doesn't fully form until about seven to 14 days after birth. Once their eyelids develop, they can open their eyes.

Blink

('bliŋk)

Like humans, cats automatically blink to moisten their eyes. But when your cat stares at you and slowly blinks, it is considered a sign of affection and an indication that it's feeling safe. Just be careful with a cat that stares at you without blinking—that could mean it's challenging you. Cats that stare at each other are negotiating. Two cats may vie for dominance and the one that blinks first loses.

Who Knew?

Comfortable cats will make direct eye contact with their owners; newly adopted or shy cats may avert their gaze to play it safe.

Blue

('blü)

Like a clear sky, blue is also the color of all kittens' eyes when they are born. That's because melanin, the pigment that gives eyes a darker hue, doesn't move into the eyes until a cat is between 7 and 12 weeks old. While breeds such as the Siamese and Himalayan continue to have blue peepers for their whole lives, most cats' eyes will turn green, brown, hazel or even yellow as they get older. More rarely, some cats have a condition called heterochromia iridis, which means each eye has a different iris color.

Who Knew?

Cats are similar to humans who are color-blind: They can see shades of blue and green, but reds, oranges, pinks and browns tend to all look the same.

Box
('bäks)

As ambush predators, cats like their own safe space to hide, so a snug box can be an ideal spot for a feline to curl up and take a nap. Researchers have found that cats in shelters with access to boxes have reduced stress and are more likely to adjust to a level of "recovery" after just two days. Of course, there's also the other kind of box, filled with litter, where cats do their bathroom business.

Who Knew?

In addition to security, boxes offer cats warmth. A National Research Council study found that domestic cats prefer temperatures between 86 F and 97 F. Curling up inside a cardboard box allows cats to generate and maintain heat.

Catnip

('kat-nip)

Want to see your kitty go crazy? Try offering it some of this psychoactive plant, which cats often react to with wanton abandonment, blissfully rolling around in it, chewing on it or just drooling when near it. A strong-scented perennial mint, catnip contains a chemical substance called nepetalactone (it's also found in some mosquito repellents!) that is not considered to be addictive or harmful —and may actually be good for bored house cats to help them stay engaged.

Who Knew?

Catnip can be used to protect your furniture if your cat is prone to scratching it: Rub some catnip on a scratching post or cat toys to divert it away from your couch.

Chirp

('chərp)

Also known as chatter or twitter, these are the birdlike sounds cats make when they're imitating prey during a hunt. Cats often vocalize this way when they're spellbound looking out the window at a squirrel or bird that sits just out of reach. The noise is different from a "trill," which is more high-pitched and can be made while a cat is playing with its human.

Who Knew?

Scientists have discovered that feral and socialized cats make different sounds, indicating humans have influenced their repertoires.

Clicker
('kli-kər)

A tool that makes a sound when you press a button and can be used to train cats. Clickers link the sound and the reward in the cat's mind. Once the cat makes that association, the clicker becomes the signal for the cat to do what you've asked, such as paw-shaking, sitting and giving you a high five. You can usually find clickers at pet stores or online for as little as $5.

Who Knew?

According to a study published in *Animals*, training has the potential "to modify unwanted behaviors and enhance the human-animal bond."

Community Cats
(kə-ˈmyü-nə-tē kats)

A group of outdoor, unowned cats that have joined together in protected working communities including barns, stables, warehouses and other places where cats hunt vermin. Cats that have not been socialized by humans remain wild, or feral. But community cats can also be former pets that became strays. Community cats often live full, healthy lives with their feline families, known as colonies.

Who Knew?

Trap-neuter-return (TNR) is a humane, effective approach to controlling the community cats' population. With it, cats are humanely trapped (with box traps), brought to a veterinarian to be spayed or neutered, vaccinated, ear-tipped (a universal sign that a community cat has been sterilized and vaccinated), then returned to their outdoor home.

Crepuscular

(kri-ˈpə-skyə-lər)

Active at dusk and dawn. Cats are primarily nocturnal, but they're also crepuscular, a holdover from their usual hunting time in the wild. At the very beginning and end of the day you'll likely find your cat running off extra energy by jumping, pouncing and playing. Try rewarding it after it does this with a little food, as if it had succeeded in a hunt! And if you're up for it, feel free to get involved with the activity. "The No. 1 form of cat enrichment is interactive playtime," says Samantha Bell, cat behavior and enrichment lead for Best Friends Animal Society in Los Angeles.

Who Knew?

Despite those energetic bursts, cats are generally pretty sedentary—they sleep an average of 15 hours a day, with some snoozing up to 20 hours a day.

Dental Care

('den-təl 'ker)

An important aspect of a cat's health, especially as it gets older. Gingivitis (inflammation of the gums; often reversible) and periodontitis (weakening of the tissue that attaches a tooth to the underlying gum and bone; typically not reversible) are among the most common concerns. Dental disease in cats can cause discomfort and can make eating painful. Veterinarians recommend cat owners brush their cat's teeth to prevent the buildup of plaque, and/or give treats designed to help with oral health.

Who Knew?

Periodontal disease affects approximately 70% of cats by the age of 3.

Divinity

(də-ˈvi-nə-tē)

The quality of being divine. The ancient Egyptians so admired felines that they became an iconic animal. Bastet, the sacred Egyptian goddess of fertility, childbirth and home, appears as a cat, modeling the creature's characteristics of "grace, fecundity and gentle care with aggression, swiftness and danger," notes Yekaterina Barbash, an Egyptologist at the Brooklyn Museum in New York. Worshippers hoping to achieve health and family—or life and protection—would appeal to Bastet. "They saw cats as having a spark of what makes divinity," notes Melinda Hartwig, curator of Egyptian art at Emory University's Michael C. Carlos Museum.

Who Knew?

In Egypt's agrarian society, cats became important to farmers by keeping away vermin.

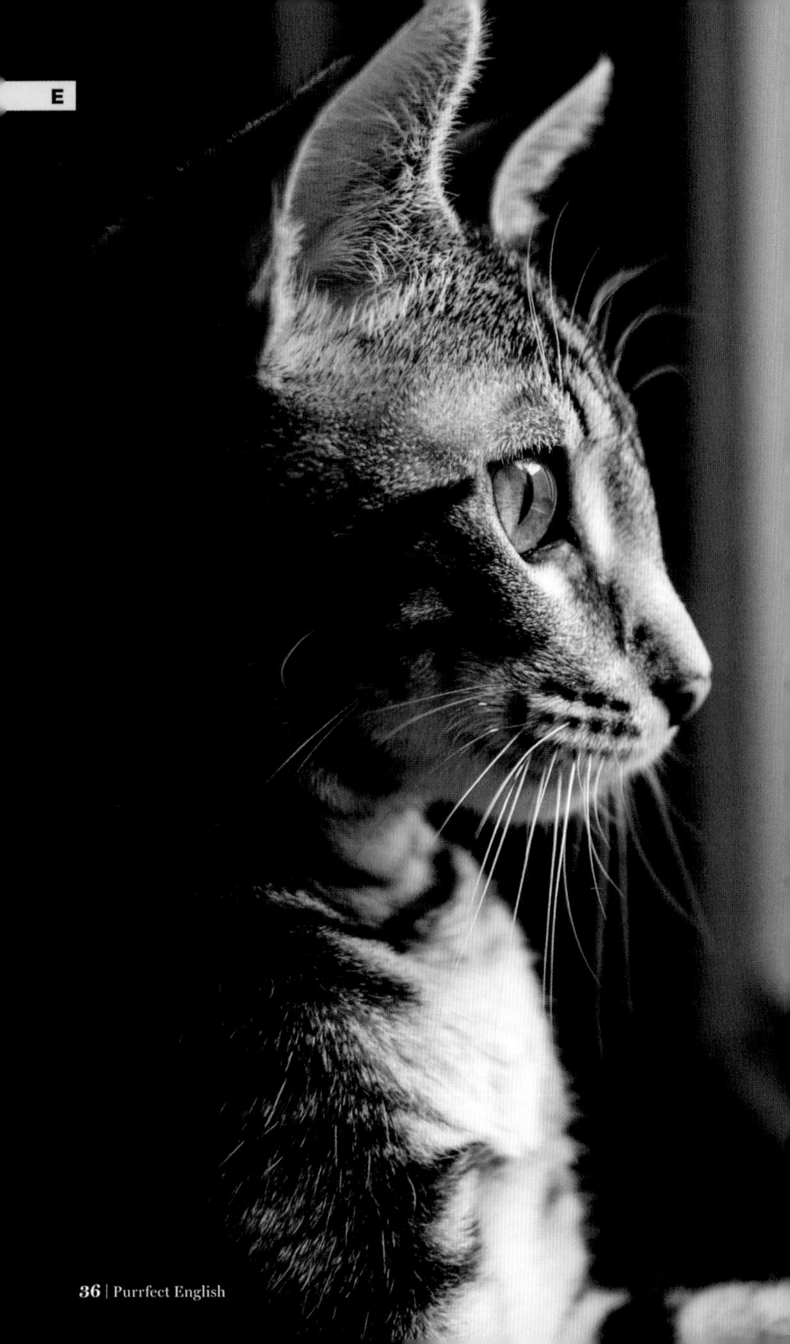

Ears
('irz)

Cats' ears give them superpower-like hearing. A cat can hear up to 64,000Hz (compared to our human listening range of up to 20,000Hz). Their ears rotate up to 180 degrees, helping them locate and identify even the faintest sounds. And credit the ears (or, more specifically, the vestibular apparatus, which sits deep inside the cat's inner ear) for the animal's amazing balance. Its tiny chambers and canals are lined with millions of fluid-filled hairs and crystals, which can rapidly signal movement to the brain regarding body positioning.

Who Knew?

Cats can hear at least one octave higher than dogs and 1.6 higher than humans.

E

Easy Listening

('ē-zē 'lis-niŋ)

Certain types of music can help cats relax, according to a study in the *Journal of Feline Medicine and Surgery.* When the animals were exposed to music specifically based on cat vocalizations such as purring and suckling, as well as frequencies similar to the feline vocal range (two octaves higher than in humans), they appeared to be less stressed during an examination compared to those that heard no music. The cat tunes were composed by David Teie, a soloist with the National Symphony Orchestra.

Who Knew?

Cat-specific music isn't the only purrfect tune: A study from the University of Lisbon found cats that heard a classical piece while under anesthesia were significantly more relaxed than those that heard a pop or a heavy metal song.

Family

('fam-lē)

A social unit living under one roof. Cats are considered to be members of the family by 99% of their owners, in large part because they help preserve our mental and physical equilibrium and play an important role in our daily lives. Cats are a constant source of kinship—and as much as we try to make them feel safe, they do the same for us.

Who Knew?

Approximately 32 million American households have at least one cat, with an average of 1.8 cats per household.

Feral

('fe-rəl)

A cat that is not domesticated; wild. Cats are considered feral if they have never been pets and live like raccoons, possums and other wild animals, roaming in the alleyways of cities or in fields in the countryside. Feral cats can benefit from being fed and from spaying/neutering efforts (TNR) to help control overpopulation, but they are generally not good rescue candidates, as they are typically too fearful to be handled or adopted. If a cat has been ear-tipped (where one ear, usually the left, has been cleanly squared off), it indicates that it's a feral cat that has been trapped before and spayed or neutered.

Who Knew?

There are an estimated 70 million feral and stray cats in the U.S.

Fight-or-Flight

(ˌfīt-ər-ˈflīt)

The instinctual reaction to a stressful situation, shared by cats and humans alike. Stress in cats can cause a variety of behavioral problems. Two of the feline's defense strategies include defensive aggression (fight) or withdrawing from the threat (flight). As they evolved, cats in the wild learned that fight-or-flight could be lifesaving, but in domesticated cats this behavior is seen as a sign of anxiety. If it becomes chronic, the stress can be unhealthy, affecting appetite, sleep and overall well-being.

Who Knew?

Cats that are highly stressed will have elevated levels of cortisol—the same hormone that humans produce when anxious or upset.

Growl

('grau(ə)l)

Rumble; to complain angrily. The growl is part of a cat's repertoire of vocalizations used to communicate aggression or defensiveness, which also includes hissing and howling. Two cats may growl at each other to determine dominance. The cat with the loudest, lowest frequency tends to win. But cats can also growl at humans as a warning noise—a signal to back off from unwanted physical contact and/or to stay away from certain toys or food.

Who Knew?

Growls are just one form of oral communication among cats; research has found up to 21 different types of feline vocalizations.

Grumpy

(ˈgrəm-pē)

A moody, cross cat. Grumpy Cat was the nickname of an American internet celebrity cat who had a permanently "grumpy" facial appearance caused by an underbite and feline dwarfism. Born in 2012, her real name was Tardar Sauce, and she became famous after the brother of her owner posted a picture of her on Reddit. She died in 2019.

Who Knew?

Dwarf cats are commonly known as munchkin cats and they are adorable, but their short legs are the result of genetic deformities that can cause mobility issues as well as heart and lung defects.

Headbutt

('hed-bət)

The action of a cat tapping its head against you or objects, such as walls, chairs and other furniture. (Animal behavioralists call this "cat bunting.") A cat headbutt is used for bonding and social purposes; it's a sign of trust. Cats only tend to do this when they're feeling safe and comfortable around their human owners.

Who Knew?

Cats have scent glands all over their bodies and bunting allows them to leave marks on objects—including their humans.

Hiss

('his)

A short, breathy sound made with an open mouth and bared teeth that indicates a cat is feeling startled and/or threatened. Spitting is a more extreme and demonstrative form of hissing. A hiss is a classic sign of feline hostility and can indicate a fight is imminent.

Who Knew?

When introducing two cats, if either cat hisses or growls, you'll need to take things slow. If the two cats don't eventually stop hissing, the pairing may not work.

Horseshoe

('hors-shü)

The shape a cat's tail can make when it is raised and tipped to the left or the right (mimicking the shape of a horseshoe). When a cat holds its tail like this, it generally indicates very friendly emotions.

Who Knew?

Cats' tails can telegraph emotions to help humans decipher how a pet is feeling. A raised tail is a friendly signal, a wagging tale indicates attention —but the more the tail wags, the more upset the cat may be.

Hunters

('hən-tərz)

A cat that hunts or pursues prey for food or sport. Hunting is one of a cat's natural instincts, and even domestic cats may hunt and kill small birds and mammals. Toys such as feather wands and cloth mice can appease your cat's need to hunt by allowing it to chase and pounce inside without harming other animals. Mealtimes can be made to gratify a cat's hunting instinct: Use food puzzles that may require some mental and physical engagement to release a treat.

Who Knew?

One big reason cats are such good hunters: They have a sense of smell that is 14 times that of humans.

Independent

(ˌin-də-ˈpen-dənt)

The state of not requiring or relying on something else. Cats need their own safe space to be left alone. While they may occasionally enjoy attention, in general their taste for human interaction has limits. And while they may enjoy some lap time, don't try to force them to stay when they are ready to go. A cat will let its human know when it's time to take off or retreat.

Who Knew?

A study in the journal *PLOS ONE* found that most cats did not show signs of missing their owners when they were left alone.

Introverted

('in-trə-ˌvər-təd)

Possessing a reserved or shy nature with an inclination toward solitude. Studies have found that people who owned cats were one-third more likely to live alone than dog owners, and twice as likely to exhibit signs of being introverted. "On average, cats are suited to providing company to a person at home engaging in solitary activities [such as reading a book]," notes Sam Gosling, PhD, a psychologist at the University of Texas in Austin.

Who Knew?

Cat owners have been found to be 12% more neurotic—and therefore more prone to anxiety and depression—than dog owners, but 11% more open than dog people, with a greater appreciation for the arts, emotion and new experiences.

Jump

('jəmp)

The act of springing into the air. Cats have an instinct to jump and leap on their prey in the wild, but they will also jump up to high places to seek safety. A combination of long limbs and powerful muscles in their back and hindquarters give the animals that extra spring. A cat will often start a jump in a deep crouch, then lift its front legs before making an "explosive extension" with its back legs, according to a study in the *Journal of Experimental Biology*. The ability to jump, turn in midair and land on one's feet is a phenomenon known in physics as "anholonomy."

Who Knew?

Cats can easily jump up to six times their own height—without a running start.

Jungle Gym

(ˈjəŋ-gəl ˈjim)

From the playground equipment of the same name, this is a household object that targets the natural inclinations and interests of cats by offering vertical space, high perches, levels to climb, resting spots, hanging objects and scratching areas. Also called a cat tree, it's designed to provide exercise, relaxation, play, security and places for your kitty to sleep or just chill out. Some jungle gyms also feature sheltered areas where a cat can hide and survey the territory below itself.

Who Knew?

Jungle gyms aren't all beige-carpeted towers— the newest designs have a more modern edge with sleeker lines and eco-friendly materials.

Juvenile

('jü-və-nī(-ə)l)

In cats, this is the age from 6 months to 2 years. During this time, the animals reach their full, adult size. Juvenile cats are just like teenagers—they have their own hormonal challenges along with some excess energy. And as with human teens, it's a developmental stage well-suited for social exploration. This is a good time to introduce juvenile cats to a variety of toys, as well as animals and other people, so they can learn and grow.

Who Knew?

Juvenile cats that are not neutered or spayed tend to roam away from their home to find a mate. This can lead to a cat becoming lost, injured or killed by cars or other wildlife.

Kibble

('ki-bəl)

Processed dry food made into tiny, uniform pieces. Kibble is usually packaged in bags, and when sealed properly, it can stay fresh for months. While convenient, kibble contains more carbohydrates than canned food, and as true carnivores, cats cannot thrive only on dietary carbs. Because kibble is dry, and many cats don't drink enough water, having it as their main food can also create health conditions such as kidney disease. And—as with humans—too many carbs can lead to obesity and diabetes.

Who Knew?

Dry kibble is better for cats' teeth, but wet food usually has a better mix of healthy ingredients. Try offering a mixture of both to your pet.

Kitten

('kit-n)

A cat that is between 4 weeks and 6 months of age (before this they are considered to be neonatal). A kitten's ear canals will begin to open at around week three; their sense of smell begins around week four. Kittens will start to stand (or wobble) at approximately 1 month old, and they will begin to explore the environment around them. Kittens ideally should be kept with their mother and littermates until they are around 8 weeks to 12 weeks old, which will help them get the nutrition they need from their mother's milk as well as early behavioral skills.

Who Knew?

A kitten's healthy weight is roughly equal to its age in months, up to about 6 months. So a 1-month-old kitten should weigh about 1 pound, and a 2-month-old kitten should weigh about 2 pounds.

Knead

('nēd)

The act of pushing in and out with the front paws, alternating between left and right. Cats usually knead on soft surfaces, such as blankets, pillows, other animals and even people. Kneading is considered a leftover behavior from infancy; as adults, cats knead to express their comfort and happiness. It's also possible that cats knead to spread their scent, because they have scent glands in the pads of their paws.

Who Knew?

Kittens knead on their mothers' breasts to express milk flow. Nursing is such a soothing experience that once cats are weaned, they continue to knead.

Language

('laŋ-gwij)

The variety of sounds that cats can produce.
These include meow variants, squeaks,
yowls, hisses, moans, chatters, howls,
trills, snarls, screeches and growls. The
volume, pitch and duration of these sounds
signify different meanings. Each cat has
a personal voice quality, varying in pitch,
tone and melody.

Who Knew?

Cats use different sounds when they communicate
with humans. Sounds that get results, such as one
that prompts their owner to feed them, are the types
that cats will keep using.

Lil Bub
(lil ˈbəb)

A domestic cat known for her unique physical appearance and made famous through social media. Lil Bub was born in Indiana in 2011 with a number of genetic mutations, including dwarfism, polydactylism and a malformed lower jaw. These conditions made her appear as a kitten well into adulthood. Lil Bub became a celebrity cat after her owner posted her videos to YouTube and they went viral. She died in December 2019.

Who Knew?

Lil Bub starred in *Lil Bub & Friendz*, a 2013 documentary about her life and other internet-famous cats; it won the Tribeca Online Festival Best Feature Film.

Mark

('märk)

To leave a scent on something to claim territory. Cats communicate largely through smells, and have scent glands in their paws, cheeks and flanks. When a cat rubs against something (or someone), it is leaving its unique scent and staking its claim to this object, person or area. Often cats will rub their cheeks against their humans as a way to mark them with their pheromones and claim them as family. Scratching is also a form of marking.

Who Knew?

Cats that mark their territory by spraying urine (something both males and females do) may be signaling one of a few different concerns, including stress, a medical problem or a dirty litter box; it may also be a mating behavior in intact cats.

Meow
(mē-ˈaů)

A specific vocalization that cats make. Meowing is an attention-seeking sound, mostly used to communicate with humans. Meows differ by loudness and softness, rising and falling melody, and duration. There are four subtypes. The mew is a high-pitched meow used when cats are distressed or need attention. The squeak is made with a more open mouth as a friendly request. A moan is a sound that rises and then falls, signaling sadness or distress. And there's the typical meow—mouth first open, then closed—which is a request for attention.

Who Knew?

The sound of meows varies with situation, need and intent, according to a study at Lund University in Sweden by phonetician Susanne Schötz.

Microchip

('mī-krō-ˌchip)

A radio-frequency identification (RFID) device the size of a grain of rice that can be implanted into a cat (or dog) just under the skin between the shoulder blades and neck to provide permanent identification, so if the animal becomes lost, it can be ID'd and returned to its owner. The microchip is activated when someone in an animal shelter or a veterinarian's office waves an RFID scanner across the area where the microchip is embedded. The microchip is made of biocompatible material so it won't cause an allergic reaction.

Who Knew?

Inserting a microchip into a cat only hurts about as much as drawing blood; typically the microchip is inserted by a vet while the cat is awake. It takes longer to fill out the registration paperwork than to actually microchip a cat!

Neonatal

(ˌnē-ō-ˈnā-təl)

The time in a cat's life from birth to 3 weeks of age. Newborn kittens are generally pretty helpless: They are born blind and deaf with their eyes and ear canals closed, and they cannot keep themselves warm. They are also unable to eliminate on their own; the mother cat cleans them with her rough tongue to stimulate digestion. At around 5 days old, they begin to hear and their eyes—initially a blue color—will begin to open. At 2 weeks old, kittens begin to develop their sense of smell.

Who Knew?

Without their mother, neonatal kittens require round-the-clock care. They must be kept warm or they will become comatose. Every two hours, they need to be fed a bottle of kitten formula.

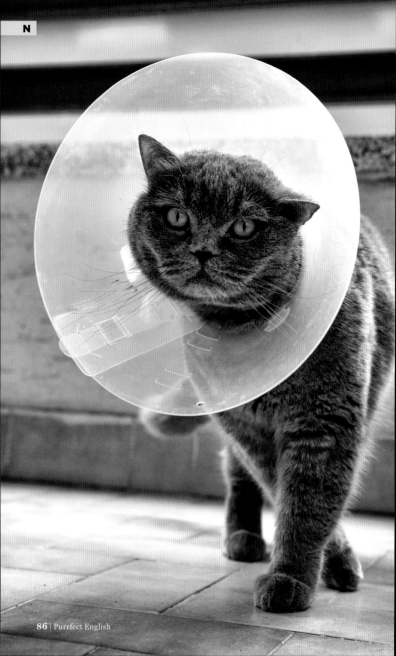

Neuter
('nü-tər)

A surgical procedure that removes the testes from a male cat. Cats that are neutered cannot reproduce. Performed under general anesthesia, the operation often takes less than two minutes, and the incision will close on its own. Healthy cats can be neutered when they are as young as 8 weeks old, as long as they weigh at least 2 pounds.

Who Knew?

In addition to population control, neutering reduces the risk of testicular and prostate cancer, urine marking, aggression and roaming behavior.

Nocturnal
(näk-'tər-nᵊl)

Active at night. Cats are primarily nocturnal animals, as anyone with a kitty that likes to zoom around in the dark well knows, but they may also display crepuscular activity (active at dawn and dusk). The good news is that domestic cats will often adjust to our schedules, preferring to share a warm bed at night. If you have a kitten or adolescent, try engaging in some interactive play an hour or so before bedtime to tire it out. But if you have an older cat that is keeping you up at night, you may need to visit the vet to rule out any health concerns.

Who Knew?

Both wild and domestic cats have built-in night vision, including a high number of rods in their retinas that allow them to see using roughly one-sixth the amount of light that humans need.

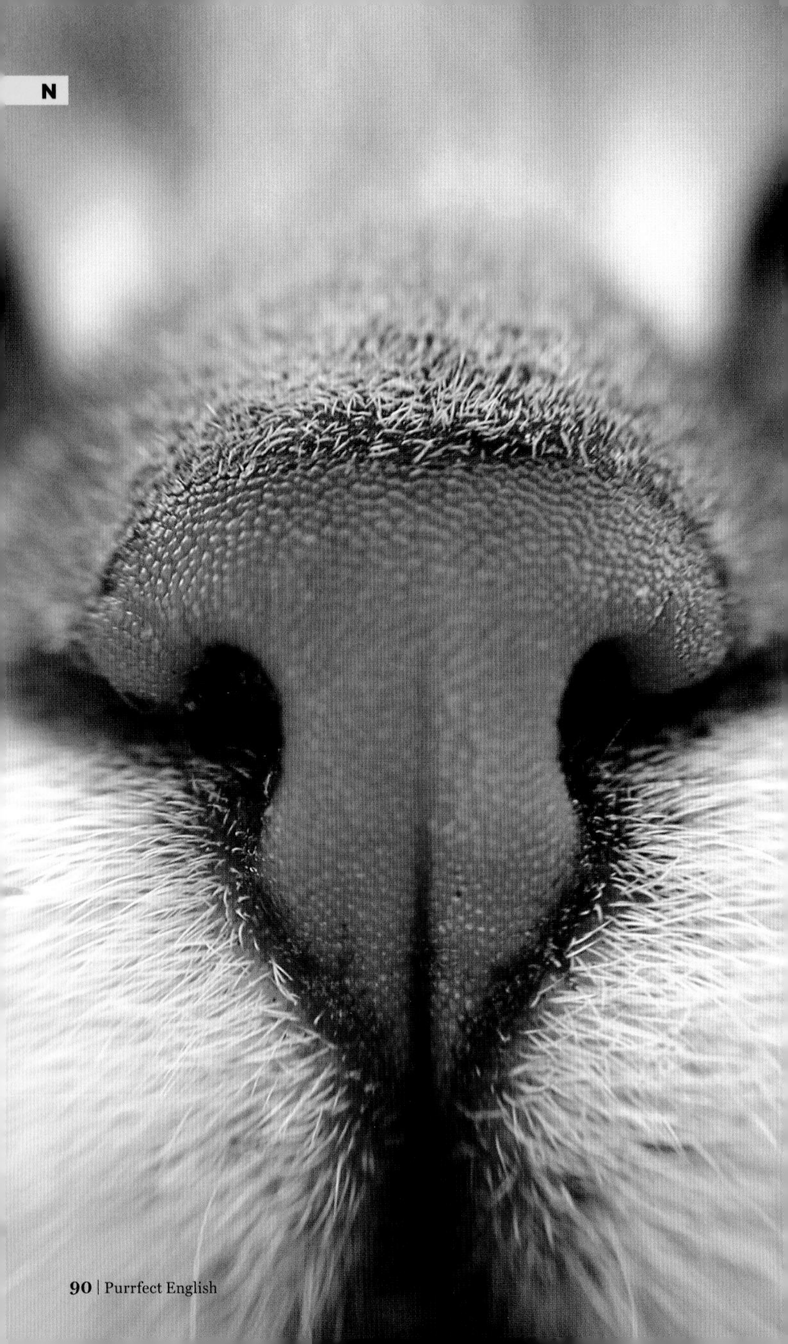

Nose

('nōz)

The part of the face that contains the nostrils and organs of smell, and functions as the passageway for air in respiration. The color of a cat's nose is related to the color of its skin: Black cats have black noses; white cats have pink noses; gray cats have gray noses; etc. Every cat's nose has a pattern of ridges and bumps, and like human fingerprints, each nose pattern is unique.

Who Knew?

Cats have more than 200 million scent receptors in their nasal cavities, compared to just 5 million in humans.

Obesity

(ō-ˈbē-sə-tē)

Obesity is the No. 1 most preventable disease of cats in the U.S. Cats are considered obese when they weigh 20% or more over their ideal weight. Like humans, obese cats are at greater risk for a variety of serious diseases, including cancer, heart disease, hypertension, diabetes, osteoarthritis, bladder stones and chronic kidney disease, among others. One major factor is the practice of "free feeding," or keeping a bowl of dry food out for your cat all day.

Who Knew?

Obesity shortens cats' life expectancy as much as 2.8 years compared to lean cats.

Oxytocin

(ˌäk-si-ˈtō-sᵊn)

A hormone secreted in the brain known as the "cuddle" or "love" chemical. Oxytocin is a neurotransmitter that enters the bloodstream and causes feelings of bonding and connection as well as positively affecting social cognition and behavior. Cats have it, and so do humans; when we spend time with our cats, our oxytocin levels rise— and vice versa. Playing with your cat can also increase two other feel-good neurochemicals, serotonin and dopamine.

Who Knew?

A study at Claremont Graduate University in California found that cats' oxytocin levels increased by 12% after playing with their owners.

Play

('plā)

Exercise or activity for enjoyment. Cats are
natural predators and play allows them to
hunt, stalk and act out other instinctive
behaviors; it also provides physical, mental
and emotional stimulation. Indoor cats
especially benefit from playing as a form of
exercise, helping them maintain a healthy
weight. Keep a variety of toys (wands, balls,
textured objects or even household objects
like paper towel rolls or water bottles) on
hand for your cat to play with, and rotate
them often to help your cat avoid boredom.

Who Knew?

Cats tend to play more when they are hungry;
hiding food around the house or using food puzzles
can entice your kitty to be more playful.

Positive Reinforcement

('pä-zə-tiv rē-ən-'fŏrs-mənt)

Presenting a motivating stimulus when a desired behavior occurs that reinforces that action. For example, use a high-value treat, a specific toy, catnip, affection or interactive play when your cat exhibits a behavior that you want to encourage. Note: For the cat to associate the reward with a specific behavior, the timing is critical. Offer the reward either simultaneously or within three seconds of the desired behavior.

Who Knew?

Positive reinforcement is much more effective than punishment or other negative stimulus, which can confuse a cat and make it fearful.

Pupil
(ˈpyü-pəl)

The elliptical vertical opening in the middle of a cat's iris that allows light to pass through the eye to the retina. As in humans, a cat's pupils constrict when the light is bright and expand when the light is low. Because cats have narrow, vertical pupils, they can expand much wider than those of most other animals, allowing them to see more clearly in the dark. Cats' pupils may also dilate when they are excited, surprised or fearful.

Who Knew?

A cat's pupils can expand up to 135 times their size (human pupils only dilate up to 15 times their size).

Purr

('pər)

The unique low-pitched vibrato sound that a cat makes with its mouth closed. Cats use both their larynx and diaphragm muscles as they inhale and exhale to produce the sound, which has a consistent pattern and frequency between 25Hz and 150Hz. While it is widely believed that cats purr when they're happy or content, cats also make this sound in a few other situations, including times of stress, when they're hungry and even when they are in pain.

Who Knew?

Research has shown that sound frequencies of 25Hz and 50Hz are associated with the promotion of bone growth and fracture healing, leading some to speculate that a cat's purr in the same frequencies can improve the healing process.

Queen
('kwēn)

An unspayed female cat of breeding age. Typically, cats begin to have estrous cycles (reproductive heat cycles) at 4 months to 12 months of age, with the average cat beginning at 6 months old. Longhaired or larger cats often begin heat cycles as late as 18 months. The estrous cycle typically lasts for three weeks, but can go as long as six weeks. Queens will not ovulate unless mating occurs, when a hormone triggers the release of eggs from the ovaries.

Who Knew?

Estrous cycles in queens are influenced by daylight, typically requiring 14 or more hours of natural or artificial light.

Quizzical

('kwi-zi-kəl)

Questioning or puzzled. When a cat tilts
its head to one side, it may appear to
be quizzical. Some animal behaviorists
maintain that when a cat tilts its head to
gaze at you, it is showing signs of affection
and love.

Who Knew?

Head-tilting can also indicate a medical condition.
Frequent head-tilting in cats may indicate a feeling
of imbalance caused by disorders of the vestibular
system, a sensory system located in the inner ear.

Rambunctious

(ram-ˈbəŋk-shəs)

Wildly active and boisterous. Cats may become overly playful when they are bored, when they want to release some pent-up energy and when they want us to play with them (often at inconvenient times, such as the wee hours of the morning). Providing cats with a variety of toys and other enrichment activities may help avoid too much unruly action.

Who Knew?

Kittens and young cats tend to have more bouts of playful rambunctiousness to release excess energy, but even older cats can have their moments of boisterous behavior.

Rub

('rəb)

The action of a cat pressing its body against its owners or other humans. Sometimes used as a form of greeting, a cat may rub against a person's legs, ankles and calves, and/or weave its body around a human's legs. A cat may also rub against a person to signal that it wants something—usually food or some attention.

Who Knew?

Cats release pheromones when they rub their body against something. Rubbing can be used for marking or to stimulate a sense of relaxation.

Shelter

('shel-tər)

A facility that houses homeless animals. Shelters provide food, water and a safe place to sleep. A shelter facility will also typically attempt to find homeless cats new homes or reunite lost cats with their owners. Public shelters are typically open access, which means they accept any animal brought in by the public or animal control. But when full, many shelters may be forced to euthanize animals to make room for incoming animals. Nonprofit and privately run shelters typically do not euthanize animals, but instead use foster networks to create space for more animals that need shelter.

Who Knew?

Every year, approximately 3.2 million cats enter the shelter system in the U.S., according to the ASPCA. Of those, around 860,000 are euthanized.

Socialization

(ˌsō-sh(ə-)lə-ˈzā-shən)

The process of familiarizing and preparing a cat to enjoy interactions and be comfortable with other animals, people, places, activities and objects. Keep the experience pleasant and positive to prevent your cat from becoming fearful and/or developing future behavioral problems. Socialization is most effective when a kitten is young (between 3 weeks and 9 weeks old is ideal), but adult cats can also be socialized after developing a bond that fosters a sense of security.

Who Knew?

Make sure your cat has a safe place to go if it becomes frightened, whether it's a crate, a carrier or a cardboard box.

Spay

('spā)

A surgical procedure that removes the reproductive tract, ovaries and uterus from a female cat (also known as an ovariohysterectomy). It is performed under general anesthesia and typically takes from 15 to 20 minutes, with the incision being closed by stitches under the skin that are eventually absorbed by the body. Most cats return home within 48 hours after surgery. Healthy cats can be spayed as young as 8 weeks old, as long as they weigh at least 2 pounds.

Who Knew?

Cats that are spayed before their first heat cycle have just a 0.5% risk of developing breast cancer later in life. Spaying also reduces a cat's lifetime risk of uterine infections.

Stare

('ster)

Make prolonged eye contact, usually without blinking. When two cats stare at each other intently, it may indicate an impending fight over territory or dominance. Cats use staring and other body language—including the position and movement of the ears, tails and torso—to communicate.

Who Knew?

Cats perceive direct, prolonged staring as a threat and can react aggressively. When a cat's body language signals stress or anger (stiff front legs; erect fur; tail held out stiff and straight, or curled around and under the body; hissing, spitting or growling) avoid making direct eye contact.

Tabby

('ta-bē)

A coat pattern in cats, including stripes, whirls, patches and dots; it is not a breed of cat. Tabby cats often have an M-shaped marking on the head just above the eyes. There are five tabby patterns: classic (a pattern of whirls); mackerel (stripes, including striped rings around the tail); spotted (spots down the back and sides); patched (patches of color, also called tortoiseshell); and ticked (tabby markings on the face and agouti hairs, which are individual hairs on the body that are striped with alternating light and dark bands).

Who Knew?

Tabby cats are domestic cats, but their DNA has been traced to ancient wildcats that inhabited North Africa and the Near East 10,000 years ago.

Tapetum Lucidum

(tə-ˈpē-təm ˈlü-si-dəm)

A layer in the part of the eye of nocturnal animals that reflects light onto the retina, allowing the animal to see better in the dark. (It also causes that spooky glowing-eyes-at-night effect.) When light enters the eye, it doesn't always hit the photoreceptors that transmit information to the brain; the tapetum lucidum acts like a mirror to bounce the light back again, giving cats and other animals with the membrane superior night vision.

Who Knew?

Cats frequently have eyes that glow bright green, but Siamese cats' eyes often glow bright yellow.

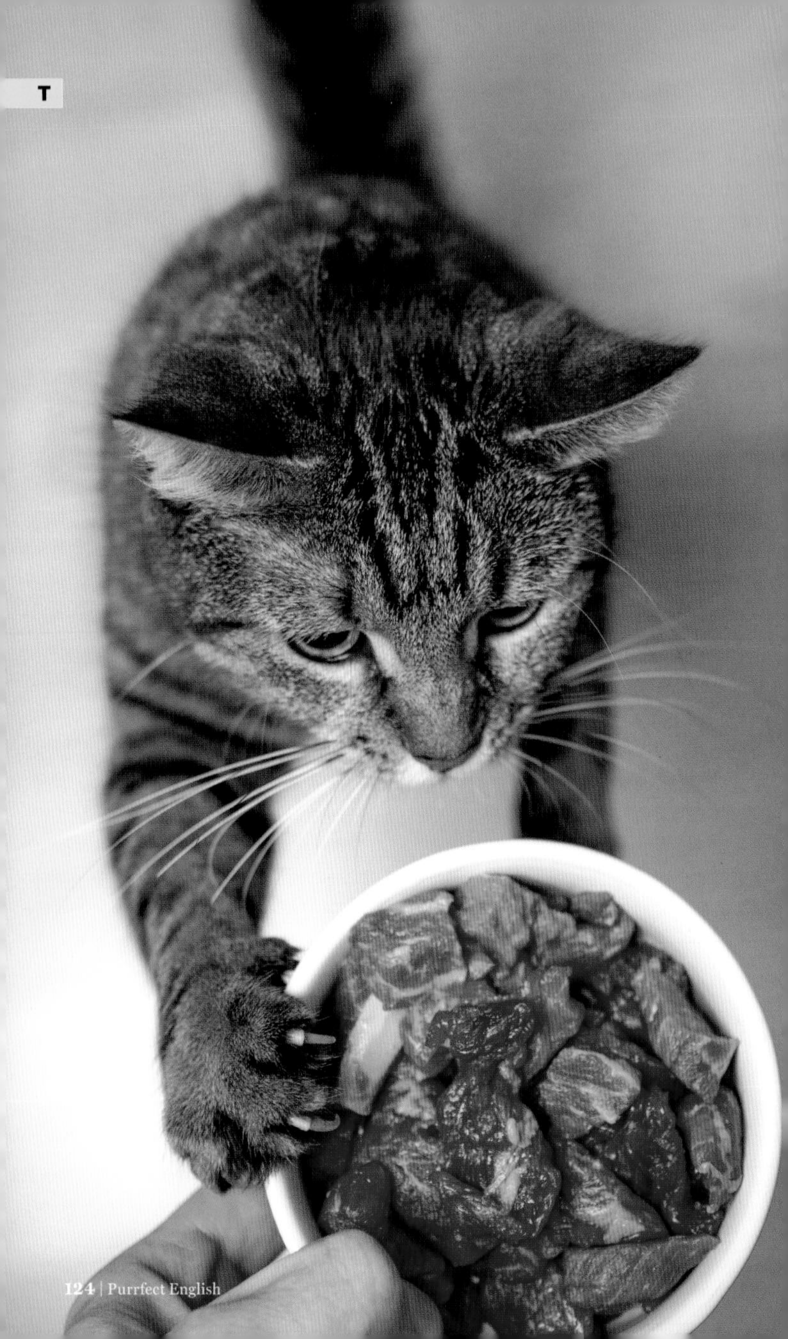

Taurine
('tȯ-rīn)

An organic compound that is considered to be an essential amino acid, which means cats cannot synthesize it. Taurine is found in animal protein, particularly in muscle, and is crucial for a variety of functions, including eyesight, digestion, immune response and the cardiovascular system. Cats that are deficient in this nutrient can develop serious conditions including blindness, dilated cardiomyopathy and immune disorders.

Who Knew?

As carnivores, cats should primarily get their nutrition from animal proteins, and the first ingredient listed on a cat food label should be meat, fish or poultry. Cats also benefit from vegetables, but no cat should be put on a fully vegetarian diet, says veterinarian Hyunmin Kim, staff manager of community medicine at the ASPCA.

Territorial

(ˌter-ə-ˈtȯr-ē-əl)

The act of claiming and defending a specific space or area. In the wild, a cat's territory is where it eats, sleeps, hunts and looks for mates. Today's indoor and outdoor cats are driven by the same possessive instincts, and can try to mark their territory by spraying urine, hissing, stalking or attacking another cat. Intact male cats are particularly territorial. Helping your cat develop socialization skills and using positive reinforcement to reward desirable behavior can help curb aggressive territorial actions.

Who Knew?

Every wild and domestic cat has a unique scent that it uses to mark its territory.

Tongue

('tən)

A cat's tongue is covered with papillae, the tiny barbs that give it its rough, sandpaper-like feel. The abrasive projections, which are sheathed with keratin (the same substance that makes your fingernails hard), give the tongue some added strength, helping to break down and digest food. They also come in handy for a cat's self-grooming sessions, untangling fur much like a comb.

Who Knew?

Cats groom with their tongues to stay clean but also to help relieve anxiety, fear and stress.

Treat

('trēt)

Small amounts of something tasty. Cat treats are available in different forms, from the packaged versions you can buy in the pet store to some simple canned tuna or cooked chicken. Use treats to reward positive behavior or just to tell your cats you love them. Just don't overdo it: Calories from treats should make up no more than about 10% of a cat's total daily caloric intake, vets say. For a 10-pound cat that needs 200 to 250 calories a day, that's only about 20 to 25 calories in the form of treats.

Who Knew?

Cats don't have the same taste buds humans do, and they can't taste anything sweet—so avoid cat treats that have added sugars.

Uncanny

(ˌən-ˈka-nē)

Possessing extraordinary sensory ability. Many of a cat's senses are dramatically greater than ours. They have nearly 40 times more odor-sensitive cells in their noses than humans, which helps them pick up vital information. Although their vision is not as attuned to distance as humans, they can see remarkably well in low-light conditions. A cat's ears can rotate 180 degrees, and cats can detect higher frequencies than dogs can. Even their whiskers can distinguish tiny changes in their environment.

Who Knew?

Some owners swear their animal has a sixth sense, and while there's not much proof, some do seem to have a special cat-person connection, as seen with cats that work with children who have autism, or those with dementia.

Unhappy

(ˌən-ˈha-pē)

The emotional state of being sad or depressed. Behaviorists sometimes call depression in cats "an absence of joy." It may manifest as subdued behavior or noticeable personality changes, such as a lack of appetite, an increase in sleeping time, a decrease in grooming (leading to a dull or matted coat), avoidance of physical contact and a loss of interest in play. Environmental changes, such as the loss of a person or another pet, or the arrival of a baby or other new pet in the household, can cause depression in cats.

Who Knew?

Some cats develop compulsive behaviors such as repeated meows, pacing back and forth, or chasing their tails. This can work as a short-term coping mechanism, but if it appears to be hurting your cat, talk to your vet.

Unlawful

(ˌən-ˈlȯ-fəl)

Not allowed by a county, state or nation. Declawing your cat—the process of amputating the last bone of each toe—is an unlawful action in some places. New York was the first state in the country to make declawing a cat, also called onychectomy, illegal. Medical issues from declawing include pain, infection, tissue death, lameness and back pain. In addition to being very painful, declawing leaves cats defenseless and can cause emotional issues such as aggression, biting and chronic stress.

Who Knew?

Declawing has been banned in most European countries, some Canadian provinces and several U.S. cities, including Denver, San Francisco and Los Angeles.

Up
(ˈəp)

Cats need their personal space—and they often find it in high spots where they can view the world below them. Seeking out high places is a protective instinct that evolved from their tree-climbing wildcat ancestors, where they could escape to safety or to lie in wait for prey. In the home, shelves and cat trees (aka jungle gyms) allow cats to relax in a quiet place and escape stressful situations.

Who Knew?

Cats have fishhook-shaped claws that help them climb trees. Unfortunately, once they're at the top, the only way to go down is backward, which they may be unwilling to do. Thus, the cat-stuck-in-the-tree scenario.

Veterinarian

(ˌve-tə-rə-ˈner-ē-ən)

A person who has been trained in the science of animal medicine. Regular preventive veterinary care—along with nutritious food, exercise and companionship—will help keep cats healthy. Cats are skilled at hiding signs of illness, so veterinarian visits are essential, providing important vaccinations, general physical exams and even dental care. Younger cats should go to a vet yearly for a wellness checkup; senior cats (those over age 8) should have semiannual visits.

Who Knew?

Veterinarians generally devote eight years to their education, including four years in college and four years in graduate school earning a degree as a doctor of veterinary medicine (DVM).

Vocalization

(ˌvō-kə-lə-ˈzā-shən)

Sounds produced with the voice. Cats' vocalizations include purring, meowing, howling, moaning, hissing, chattering, trilling, chirping, squeaking, mating calls and moaning. When a cat uses vocalizations to communicate with humans, it usually means it wants you to do something, or it wants you to stop doing something.

Who Knew?

It's not just the noise a cat makes that can indicate its mood: You also need to read a cat's body language (from whiskers to tail) to get a full indication of what it's trying to say.

Wands

('wändz)

Wands are interactive toys that provide cats with both mental and physical exercise, helping to strengthen your kitty-human bond, while also boosting a cat's confidence and giving indoor cats the opportunity to engage in instinctual hunting activity. Wands are generally constructed using a long, often flexible pole that has a string on one end with an object (often feathers or a small toy) attached to it. When waved through the air, it appears to cats as prey.

Who Knew?

Use a wand to teach your cat how to high five: When it raises its paw to reach for the toy, give it a reward. (You may need to move the toy around a bit to get a cat to reach toward it.) Once your cat associates the pawing motion with a treat, decrease the wand movement. Eventually, you can move the wand out of the way so your cat reaches for your hand.

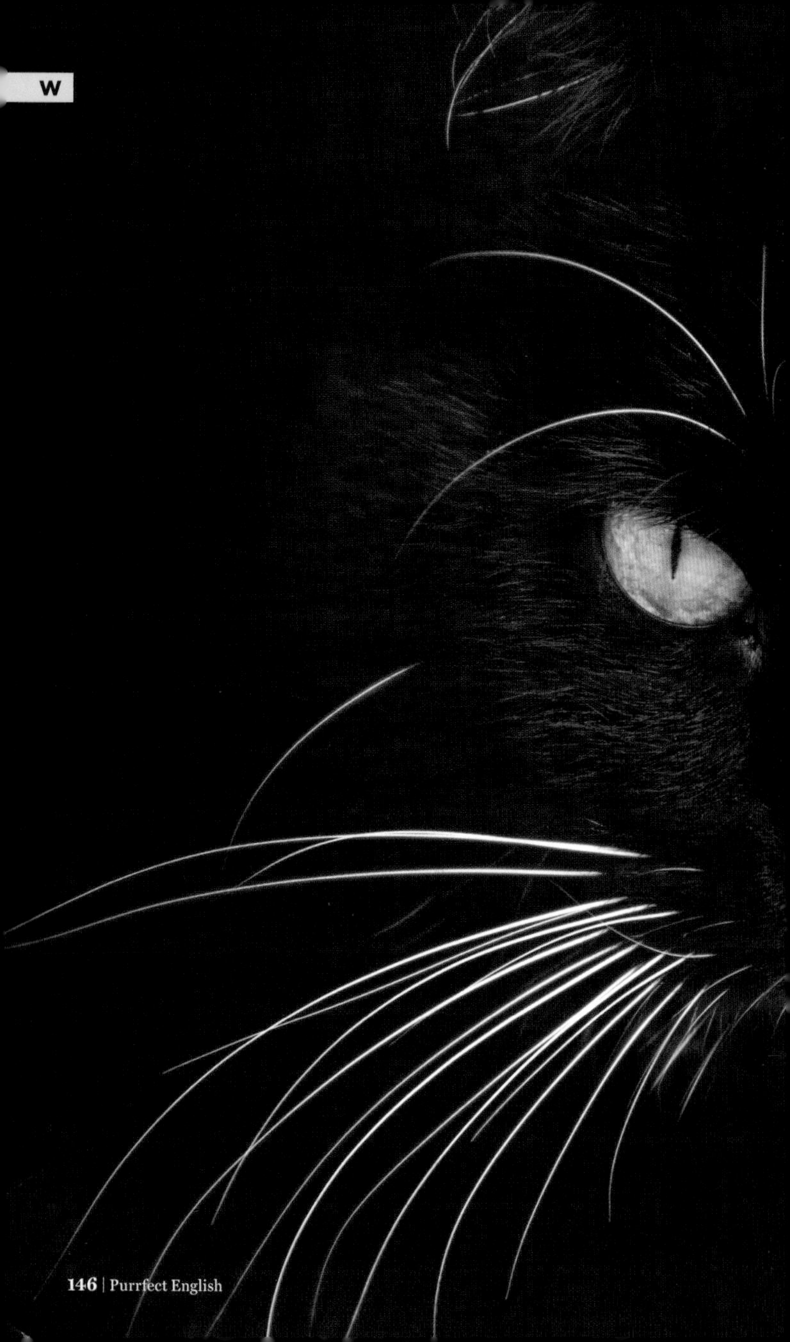

Whiskers

('wi-skərz)

The long, stiff hairs that grow at the sides of a cat's mouth, above its eyes and elsewhere on its body. Whiskers are sensitive and tactile, and they can detect subtle changes in the environment. Whiskers that are bent back indicate anxiety or discomfort; whiskers bent forward mean that the cat is at attention. By brushing its whiskers against an object, a cat can detect its precise location, size and texture.

Who Knew?

Cats' whiskers, also known as "vibrissae," enhance the feline sense of balance.

Wildcats

(ˈwī(-ə)l(d)-ˌkatz)

Punctuation is important here: Wild cats (two words) are feral cats; wildcats (one word) are a distinctive small cat species, like the lynx, from North Africa, Europe and North America. Our modern house cats have very few genetic differences from these wildcats—there are as few as 13 genes with significant variations between the wild and domesticated species, according to a study in *Proceedings of the National Academy of Sciences*. The main difference: an ability to get along with people.

Who Knew?

All domestic cats are descended from a single subspecies of wildcat—*Felis silvestris lybica*—the Near Eastern wildcat, according to a study in the journal *Science*.

X-Ray Vision

(ˈeks-ˌrā ˈvi-zhən)

The ability to see through something. Cats have the ability to see through the dark. This is due to the vertical, elliptical shape of their pupils, which can dilate much wider than most animals to let in more light. Cats also have two kinds of light-detecting cells, called cones and rods. Cones distinguish colors, and rods respond to light intensity. Cats have between five and six times more rods than humans have. The many rods in a cat's retina also serve as motion detectors, helping a cat quickly detect any object that moves across its field of vision.

Who Knew?

Cats can see in as little as one-sixth the light that humans need.

Y

Yowl

(ˈyau̇(-ə)l)

Making a long, loud call that sounds distressed. Cats may yowl when they are depressed or ill. Yowling can indicate pain, discomfort, hunger or a negative reaction to something in the environment. It's often a cat-to-cat communication, indicating either the desire to mate or to claim territory. However, it can also be a sign of dementia in senior cats that may cry out for unknown reasons.

Who Knew?

Several factors can help interpret a cat's yowling, including the environment, the situation and the animal's body language.

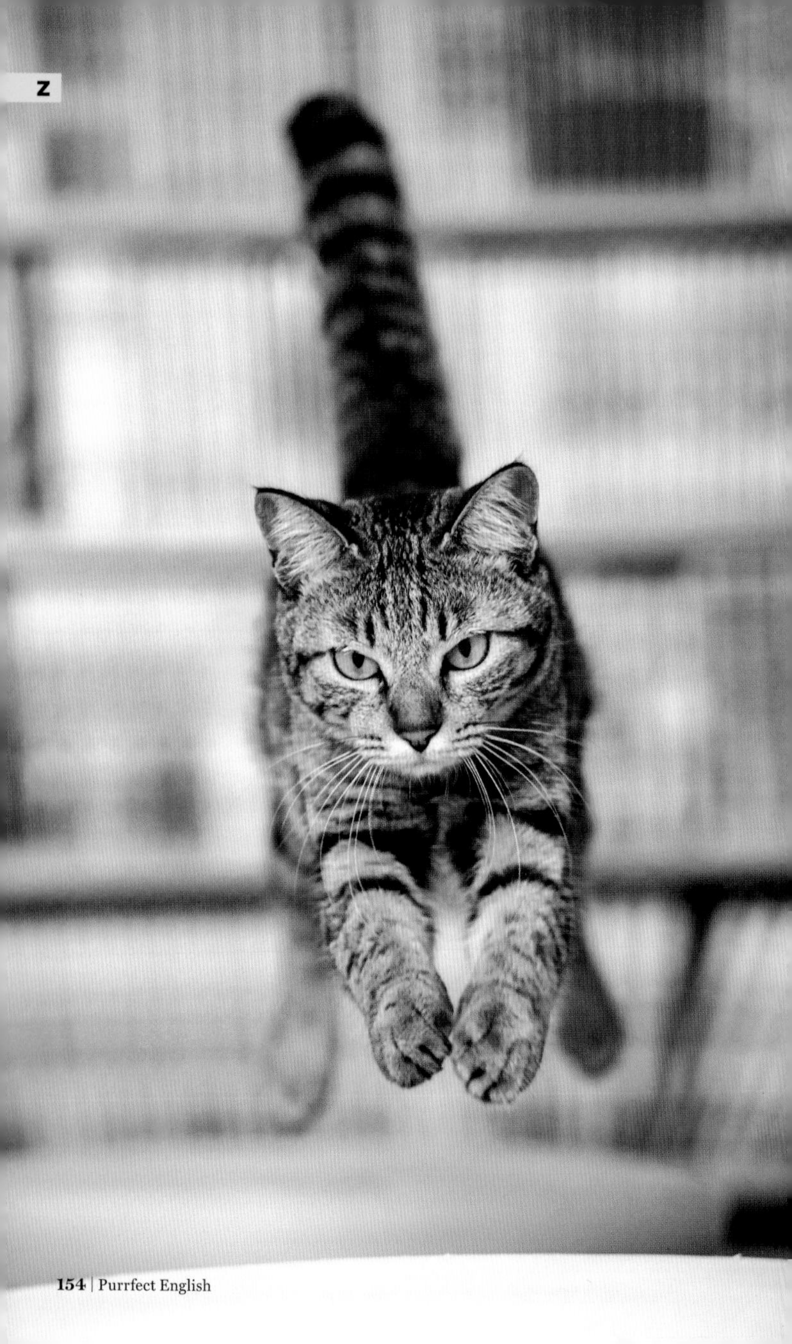

Zoom

('züm)

Periods of hyperactivity when cats race around, erratically stopping and starting. Also known as the "zoomies," cats run around wildly to release excess energy. Because cats are largely nocturnal, the zoomies occur frequently at night when they would naturally be hunting. Zooming is a normal activity, but if it's accompanied by weight loss, changes in litter box usage or unusual vocalization, consult your veterinarian.

Who Knew?

The clinical term for zoomies is frenetic random activity periods, or FRAPs.

INDEX

INDEX

CREDITS

SPECIAL THANKS TO CONTRIBUTING WRITER

Pamela Weintraub

CENTENNIAL BOOKS

An Imprint of
Centennial Media, LLC
40 Worth St., 10th Floor
New York, NY 10013, U.S.A.

ISBN 978-1-951274-74-0

Distributed by
Simon & Schuster, Inc.
1230 Avenue of the Americas
New York, NY 10020, U.S.A.

For information about custom editions, special sales and
premium and corporate purchases, please contact Centennial Media
at contact@centennialmedia.com.

Manufactured in China

Publishers & Co-Founders Ben Harris, Sebastian Raatz
Editorial Director Annabel Vered
Creative Director Jessica Power
Executive Editor Janet Giovanelli
Features Editor Alyssa Shaffer
Deputy Editors Ron Kelly, Anne Marie O'Connor
Managing Editor Lisa Chambers
Design Director Martin Elfers
Senior Art Director Pino Impastato
Art Directors Natali Suasnavas, Joseph Ulatowski
Copy/Production Patty Carroll, Angela Taormina
Assistant Art Director Jaclyn Loney
Senior Photo Editor Jenny Veiga
Photo Editor Kate Mix
Production Manager Paul Rodina
Production Assistant Alyssa Swiderski
Editorial Assistant Tiana Schippa
Sales & Marketing Jeremy Nurnberg